TABLE OF C

➦►◆◄

CHAPTER   PAGE

Unless otherwise indicated, all Scripture quotations are taken from the *King James Version* of the Bible.
Seeds of Wisdom on Goal-Setting
ISBN 1-56394-133-3
Copyright © 2001 by *MIKE MURDOCK*
All publishing rights belong exclusively to Wisdom International
Published by The Wisdom Center · P. O. Box 99 · Denton, Texas 76202
1-888-WISDOM-1 (1-888-947-3661) · Website: www.thewisdomcenter.cc

Stop Looking At
Where You Have Been
And Start Looking At
Where You Can Be.

-MIKE MURDOCK

❦ 1 ❦

GOAL-SETTING IS WRITING DOWN ANYTHING YOU WANT TO BECOME, DO OR HAVE.

――――▶⊙◀――――

You Can Only Do Something You Can See.

You must *see* a goal—before you can *reach* it. You must see it in The World of Your Experience or, The Room of Your Imagination. God explained this phenomenon in Genesis. When the arrogant government leaders decided to build a monument to themselves that would reach the Heavens...God came down to stop it. Yet, He acknowledged the Law of Visualization and its potential. "...now nothing will be restrained from them, which they have imagined to do" (Gen. 11:6).

10 Facts About Setting Goals

1. *God Knows Your Desires And Needs.* "...for your Heavenly Father knoweth that you have need of all these things" (Matt. 6:32).

2. *God Wants Those Dreams And Goals To Happen.* "Delight thyself also in the Lord; and He shall give thee the desires of thine heart" (Ps. 37:4).

3. *God Expects You To Document Those Desires By Writing Them Down As A Covenant Between You And Him.* "Write the vision, and make it plain upon tables, that he may run that readeth it" (Hab. 2:2).

4. *God Will Impart The Divine Schedule And Plan For The Achieving Of Your Goal.* "For the vision is yet for an appointed time, but at the end it shall speak, and not lie: though it tarry, wait for it; because it will surely come, it will not tarry" (Hab. 2:3).

5. *God Wrote His Own Goals And Dreams Down In The Word.* "For I know the thoughts that I think toward you, saith the Lord, thoughts of peace, and not of evil, to give you an expected end" (Jer. 29:11).

6. *God Plans The Entry Of Leaders Years Before Their Birth On The Earth.* "Before I formed thee in the belly, I knew thee; and before thou camest forth out of the womb I sanctified thee, and I ordained thee a prophet unto the nations" (Jer. 1:5).

7. *God Even Wrote Down His Commands And Rewards On Tables Of Stone For Moses And The Israelites.* "And I will write on the tables the words that were in the first tables which thou brakest, and thou shalt put them in the ark" (Deut. 10:2).

8. *Uncommon Leaders Know The Power Of Writing Down Events, Truths Or Covenant For The Purpose Of Destiny.* "And the Lord said unto Moses, Write this for a memorial in a book, and rehearse it in the ears of Joshua:" (Ex. 17:14).

9. *Uncommon Prophets Were Instructed To Write Down What Was Worthy Of Focus.* "Now go, write it before them in a table, and note it in a book, that it may be for the time to come for ever and ever:" (Isa. 30:8).

10. *Uncommon Leaders Were Commanded To Write Any Instruction They Received From God.* "Thus speaketh the Lord God of Israel, saying, Write thee all the words that I have spoken unto thee in a book" (Jer. 30:2).

Take a moment to review the habits of Uncommon Financial Leaders here in our generation. The late

Mary Kay Ash, a beautiful business leader, had the remarkable habit of writing down her daily goals—six things she would do that very day. She wrote them down in the order and sequence of their priority or value. Her business was valued at over 1 billion at her death.

3 Goal Sheets

Here are 3 different pages awaiting your personal investment of time, to document your goals... anything you want to become, do or have.

First: *Your Lifetime Dreams And Goals.*

You may dream of...owning your own business, traveling throughout the world, losing 40 pounds, learning a new language, being debt-free, becoming a missionary. Write it down...in detail.

Second: *Your 12-Month Goals.*

Anything you want to begin or finish within this next year. It may be to purchase your house, pay your car off, memorize a Scripture a day or lose 20 pounds.

Third: *Your 30-Day Goals.*

These may include the simple tasks of organizing your mail, cleaning out your closet, returning phone calls, meeting with your financial planner or reading a specific book you have laid to the side.

I read recently that only 3 percent of the United States population have a written list of their dreams and goals. This may explain why 3 percent govern the other 97 percent...3 percent own as much real estate as the remaining 97 percent combined and...the same 3 percent possess as much wealth as the remaining 97 percent *combined.*

Goals matter.

Written goals matter more.

YOUR LIFETIME DREAMS AND GOALS

You may dream of...owning your own business, traveling throughout the world, losing 40 pounds, learning a new language, being debt-free, becoming a missionary. Write it down...in detail.

1._____

2._____

3._____

4._____

5._____

6._____

7._____

8._____

9._____

10._____

11._____

12._____

13._____

14._____

YOUR 12-MONTH GOALS

Anything you want to begin or finish within this next year. It may be to purchase your house, pay your car off, memorize a Scripture a day or lose 20 pounds. Write it down.

1._____

2._____

3._____

4._____

5._____

6._____

7._____

8._____

9._____

10._____

11._____

12._____

13._____

14._____

YOUR 30-DAY GOALS

These may include the simple tasks of organizing your mail, cleaning out your closet, returning phone calls, meeting with your financial planner or reading a specific book you have laid to the side.

1._____

2._____

3._____

4._____

5._____

6._____

7._____

8._____

9._____

10._____

11._____

12._____

13._____

14._____

2

YOU ARE ONLY QUALIFIED FOR THE GOALS YOU ARE WILLING TO PURSUE.

────────◆───────

The Proof of Desire Is Pursuit.

You rarely reach for what you really need.

You will always reach for what you desire.

Many were blind during the time of Christ. But, remember the blind man who cried out even louder after being warned by others to be quiet.

Passion pursues.

One woman who had an issue of blood for 12 years pressed through the crowd. Nobody else cared. But, her passion to be healed birthed tenacity, determination and focus. She *received* (see Matt. 9:20-22).

God often births Faith-Pictures in your heart. We call them *miracles*. He desires to impart blessings He wants you to possess. But, it is your own personal responsibility to *pursue* for the receiving of those dreams and goals.

God does not respond to *pain*.

God only responds to *pursuit*.

Millions have not grasped this. The whining, complaining and critical unbelieving crowd accuses God continually of not truly caring. You have heard it everywhere..."Why did God let those people die of famine? Why did God permit that tragedy to happen?" While none of us truly understand all the ways of God, we do know that "...no good thing will He withhold from them that walk uprightly" (Ps. 84:11).

Reaching Is The Proof Of Humility. The proud withdraw from God. They receive nothing. The humble *reach*...pursue...because they discern God as the True Source of their desired Dream. "...for he that cometh to God must believe that He is, and that He is a rewarder of them that diligently seek Him" (Heb. 11:6).

God Requires Your Pursuit To Even Receive His Forgiveness And Mercy. "Come now, and let us reason together, saith the Lord: though your sins be as scarlet, they shall be as white as snow; though they be red like crimson, they shall be as wool" (Isa. 1:18).

You Are Not Qualified To Receive From God Until You Ask And Pursue In Faith And Confidence. "But without faith it is impossible to please Him; for he that cometh to God must believe that He is, and that He is a rewarder of them that diligently seek Him" (Heb. 11:6).

God Always Favors The Aggressive And Persistent. One of the greatest pictures was recorded by Matthew: "And, behold, a woman of Canaan came out of the same coasts, and cried unto Him, saying, Have mercy on me, O Lord, Thou Son of David; my daughter is grievously vexed with a devil. But He answered her not a word. And His disciples came and besought Him, saying, Send her away; for she crieth after us. But He answered and said, I am not sent but unto the lost sheep of the house of Israel. Then came she and worshipped him, saying, Lord, help me. But He answered and said, It is not meet to take the children's bread, and to cast it to dogs. And she said, Truth, Lord: yet the dogs eat of the crumbs which fall from their masters' table. Then Jesus answered and said unto her, O woman, great is thy faith: be it unto thee even as thou wilt. And her daughter was made whole from that very hour" (Matt. 15:22-28).

Nobody Else Is Responsible For Motivating Or Encouraging You. So, learn to encourage yourself. This was one of the Secrets of David. "Delight thyself also in the Lord; and He shall give thee the desires of thine heart" (Ps. 37:4).

The Holy Spirit documented this quality of David. "And David was greatly distressed;...but David encouraged himself in the Lord" (1 Sam. 30:6).

3 Keys To Developing Your Passion

1. *Abandon Any Dream Or Goal That No Longer Generates Joy Or Energy.* It may be a childhood fantasy, or something others thought you should pursue. But, your goals should birth enthusiasm in *you.*

2. *Pursue Goals That Qualify For Your Total Focus.* Things that truly matter deserve quality hours. Eliminate the part-time interests.

3. *Study The Habits Of Uncommon Achievers.* Thomas Edison said his difference from others was that others thought on many things while he "thought on only one thing all day long."

Jesus focused on His Assignment. "For the Son of man is come to seek and to save that which was lost" (Lk. 19:10). Paul wrote, "...I press toward the mark for the prize of the high calling of God in Christ Jesus" (Phil. 3:14).

You Are Only Qualified For The Goals You Are Willing To Pursue.

Every Relationship
In Your Life
Will Make A Deposit
Or A Withdrawal.

-MIKE MURDOCK

❧ 3 ❧

YOUR GOAL WILL REQUIRE A VARIETY OF RELATIONSHIPS.

You Cannot Succeed Alone.

The Scriptures teach the necessity of others. "Two are better than one; because they have a good reward for their labour. For if they fall, the one will lift up his fellow: but woe to him that is alone when he falleth; for he hath not another to help him up" (Eccl. 4:9-10).

Jesus did not attempt to reach the world alone. He sent them out two by two. "After these things the Lord appointed other seventy also, and sent them two and two before his face into every city and place, whither He Himself would come" (Lk. 10:1).

4 Relationships You Need To Achieve Your Goals

1. *You Will Need A Circle Of Counsel.* "Where no counsel is, the people fall: but in the multitude of counsellers there is safety" (Prov 11:14).

Focus Always Creates Blindness.

So, you must have others who see what you cannot see. Every king and world leader selects his personal Circle of Counsel, to increase the quality of his decision-making.

2. *You Will Need Uncommon Mentors.* Mentors are not simply teachers—Mentors are *trusted*

teachers. Elisha was mentored by Elijah. Timothy was mentored by Paul.

The Quality Of The Mentor Determines The Productivity Of The Protégé. One way to predict someone's future is to discern who is mentoring them. Your Mentor recognizes your Enemy before you do. Mordecai was aware of Haman before Esther even knew the evil plot herself. "And Mordecai told him of all that had happened unto him, and of the sum of the money that Haman had promised to pay to the king's treasuries for the Jews, to destroy them" (Esth. 4:7).

Cheerleaders are wonderful, but coaches win games. Correction Is As Necessary As Comfort. Every achiever knows this.

3. *You Will Need Intercessors.* Queen Esther was a beautiful woman who was the confidante of the king. But, when she focused on the goal of saving her own people she did not rely on her beauty, personality nor even her access to the king. She called a group to fast and pray. "Go, gather together all the Jews that are present in Shushan, and fast ye for me, and neither eat nor drink three days, night or day: I also and my maidens will fast likewise; and so will I go in unto the king, which is not according to the law: and if I perish, I perish" (Esth. 4:16).

4. *You Will Need Encouragers.* That is why the Scriptures instruct us to build up each other. "Brethren, if a man be overtaken in a fault, ye which are spiritual, restore such an one in the spirit of meekness; considering thyself, lest thou also be tempted. Bear ye one another's burdens, and so fulfil the law of Christ" (Gal. 6:1,2).

Your Top 7 Checklist

Take a moment to write down:

1. The Top 7 Names Of Those Who Have Consistently Expressed Personal Confidence In You And Your Dreams.

2. The Top 7 Achievers You Know Personally Who Have Achieved Uncommon Goals.

3. The Top 7 Intercessors Who Have A Strong Relationship With The Holy Spirit.

4. The Top 7 Mentors Who Are Qualified To Bring The Gift Of Correction Into Your Life.

Are you wise? Are you a fool? It is easy to recognize. The Scriptures reveal the method for discerning the *quality* of your own heart: "Reprove not a scorner, lest he hate thee: rebuke a wise man, and he will love thee" (Prov. 9:8).

Pursue these relationships. Listen to their counsel. Open your heart up and share the goals that burn within you. You will take giant steps toward your goals when you dare to reach out to involve others.

Your Goal Will Require A Variety Of Relationships.

Recommended Books And Tapes

B-11   Dreams Seeds (112 Page Book/$9)
B-14   Seeds of Wisdom on Relationships (32 Page Book/$3)
TS-11   Dream Seeds (6 Tape Series/30)
TS-63   The Uncommon Mentor (6 Tape Series/$30)

The Atmosphere
You Create Determines
The Product
You Produce.

-MIKE MURDOCK

❧ 4 ❧

YOUR GOAL IS WORTH ANY INVESTMENT NECESSARY TO CREATE THE ATMOSPHERE THAT KEEPS YOU MOTIVATED.

━━━━━━▷❂◁━━━━━━

Staying Inspired Is Often Your Greatest Battle.

Every dreamer encounters despondency. There are days of great progress and hope. Then, there are seasons of unending frustrations, delays and self-doubts. Some of the great world leaders, such as Winston Churchill and Abraham Lincoln, fought seasons of severe depression. Scriptures are filled with such moments in the lives of powerful spiritual leaders.

Jonah wanted to die after his great revival in Nineveh. "And it came to pass, when the sun did arise, that God prepared a vehement east wind; and the sun beat upon the head of Jonah, that he fainted, and wished in himself to die, and said, It is better for me to die than to live" (Jonah 4:8).

Jesus experienced great heartache. He cried out in the Garden of Gethsemane, "Father, if Thou be willing, remove this cup from Me: nevertheless not My will, but Thine, be done. And there appeared an angel unto Him from Heaven, strengthening Him. And being in an agony He prayed more earnestly: and His sweat was as it were great drops of blood falling down to the ground" (Lk. 22:42-44).

Accept such seasons as Moments of Motivation for Pursuing the Mentorship of the Holy Spirit.

1. *Anticipate The Erratic Emotional Waves That Dash Against You.* It is normal for those pursuing worthy and uncommon goals.

2. *Identify Your Personal Sources Of Enthusiam.* You may require a specific type of music. Identify it. I like waterfalls, candles and soft music. I require a peaceful climate. Others may need a loud, boisterous atmosphere to unlock their passion and enthusiasm. Invest the time necessary to think this through for yourself and your specific or changing needs.

3. *Invest In Any Equipment, Furnishings, Clothing Or Tools That Will Sculpture The Atmosphere That Feeds Your Enthusiasm And Passion.* A few days ago, I explained this to a young protégé. He was puzzled by my purchasing a new laptop. "But, you already have a very nice laptop," he said.

"Son, the new one contains the full wireless capabilities inside, contains a second back-up battery and has double the memory for all my Wisdom Files. It has the newest programs, the infrared, the serial and USB ports," I explained.

His goal was to save *money*.

My goal was to save *time*.

His goal was to *accumulate*.

My goal was to *accomplish*.

My enthusiasm, energy and passion is worth far more than $3,500. So, I was willing to invest whatever it takes to feed my joy...my energy...because money is far easier to replace than motivation and passion.

Lost money can be regained...when you are

motivated.

If you lose motivation, you lose *everything.*

I don't like cheap candles that burn without a strong fragrance. I invest in candles that fill up the room with a heavenly aroma!

The atmosphere is worth the cost.

My goal is worth the investment.

Nobody else can do this for you. So, invest whatever is necessary to protect your focus and create the climate that keeps you continually inspired and energized.

Your Goal Is Worth Any Investment Necessary To Create The Atmosphere That Keeps You Motivated.

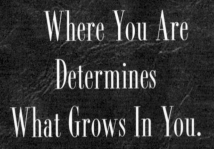

Where You Are
Determines
What Grows In You.

-MIKE MURDOCK

∾ 5 ∾

YOUR TIME IN THE SECRET PLACE WILL EXPOSE ANY POTENTIAL PITFALL IN THE PURSUIT OF YOUR GOALS.

Every Pitfall Is Avoidable.

You can eliminate ten thousand heartaches and tears by listening to the Voice of the Spirit. The cry of Jesus was to "hear what the Spirit saith" (Rev. 3:22).

The Role Of The Holy Spirit Is To Protect You. That was evident when the Holy Spirit used Agabus to warn of approaching catastrophe. "And there stood up one of them named Agabus, and signified by the Spirit that there should be great dearth throughout all the world: which came to pass in the days of Claudius Caesar" (Acts 11:28).

The Holy Spirit Discerns The Hidden Motives And Unspoken Agendas Of Others. Deception is deadly.

One Person in your life can create 20 years of tears.

One Trap can destroy a thousand dreams God desires for you.

One Lie can devastate the most noble goal and dream. Time with the Holy Spirit is the *greatest investment of your life.* "Likewise the Spirit also helpeth our infirmities: for we know not what we should pray for as we ought: but the Spirit (Himself) maketh intercession for us with groanings which cannot be uttered" (Rom. 8:26).

The Holy Spirit Anticipates The Adversarial Atmosphere You Will Enter Today. The ungodly reign...for the present. Traps are set. Poisonous arrows are in the bows of your enemies. You need a Defense. The most qualified Defense is the Master Mentor who provides The Wisdom of The Word...He will become an Enemy to your enemies! "...and vexed His Holy Spirit: therefore He was turned to be their enemy, and He fought against them" (Isa. 63:10)

The most memorable day of my life was Wednesday, July 13, 1994...the day I fell in love with the Holy Spirit. He radically changed my life...my focus...my plans. He became my Obsession, The Love of my life. I would trade every discovery of my life for what I have discovered about Him. He is The Comforter, The Spirit of Wisdom and The One Who Stayed. "And I will pray the Father, and He shall give you another Comforter, that He may abide with you for ever;" (Jn. 14:16).

▶ You must *know* Him—not merely experience Him.

▶ You must *sit* at His feet—not merely touch Him.

▶ You must establish The Secret Place...a private Room of Solitude where you meet with Him daily.

1. *Enter The Secret Place Singing To Him* (see Ps. 100:2). Love Him. Worship Him. Bishop David Oyedepo spoke this to me while I was having lunch in his home in Lagos, Nigeria. "Gratitude provokes joy.

Joy provokes praise. Your praise creates Divine Presence."

2. *Enter The Same Time Each Morning.* Habit is a gift from God. Habit takes you further than desire. It is your appointment with The Spirit of Wisdom.

3. *Stay In His Presence Long Enough To Create A Memory.* The prodigal son lost finances, friends, favor and influence...but, satan could not steal his memories.

4. *Keep A Daily Wisdom Journal.* Document His Master Secrets to you. Your success matters to Him.

Your Time In The Secret Place Will Expose Any Potential Pitfall In The Pursuit Of Your Goals.

RECOMMENDED BOOKS

B-100   The Holy Spirit Handbook, Vol. 1 (152 Page Book/$10)
B-115   Seeds Of Wisdom On The Secret Place (32 Page Book/$5)
B-116   Seeds Of Wisdom On The Holy Spirit (32 Page Book/$5)

Anything Good
Is Hated By
Everything Evil.

-MIKE MURDOCK

≈ 6 ≈

YOU MUST IDENTIFY ADVERSARIAL RELATIONSHIPS THAT DISTRACT YOU FROM YOUR GOALS.

You Will Always Have An Enemy.

Jesus had enemies and the servant is not above his lord. He instructed us to expect adversaries. "Blessed are ye, when men shall hate you, and when they shall separate you from their company, and shall reproach you, and cast out your name as evil, for the Son of man's sake" (Lk. 6:22).

5 Ways To Identify An Enemy To Your Goals

1. *An Enemy Is Anyone Who Weakens Your Influence With Others.* Nehemiah faced this. Ezra experienced it also. "...hired counsellors against them, to frustrate their purpose," (Ezra 4:5).

2. *An Enemy Is Anyone Who Focuses On Your Past Instead Of Your Future.* "Remember ye not the former things, neither consider the things of old. Behold, I will do a new thing; now it shall spring forth; shall ye not know it? I will even make a way in the wilderness, and rivers in the desert" (Isa. 43:18,19).

3. *An Enemy Is Anyone Who Attempts To Weaken Your Passion Through Contempt Or Criticism.* Nehemiah experienced this from Tobiah who sneered

at the quality of the walls being rebuilt. "Now Tobiah the Ammonite was by him, and he said, Even that which they build, if a fox go up, he shall even break down their stone wall" (Neh. 4:3).

4. *An Enemy Is Anyone Who Thinks You Are Unworthy Of Achieving A God-Given Goal.* Jesus experienced this continually from those who felt nothing good could come from Nazareth. "Is not this the carpenter, the son of Mary, the brother of James, and Joses, and of Juda, and Simon? and are not His sisters here with us? And they were offended at Him" (Mk. 6:3).

5. *Your Enemy Is Anyone Who Knowingly Distracts You From Your Goal.* Distraction Is Always The Goal Of An Adversary.

Remember this, The Only Reason Men Ever Fail Is...*Broken Focus.* Discern this. Move swiftly to protect your focus.

Special Reminders...

▶ *Your Enemy May Exist In Your Own Home.*

Jesus warned us of this possibility. "And a man's foes shall be they of his own household" (Matt. 10:36).

▶ *Fatigue Is An Enemy To Your Goal.*

Tired eyes never see a great future. God rested...on the seventh day. Jesus commanded His disciples to come apart from the crowds and the activities pressing them. "And He said unto them, Come ye yourselves apart into a desert place, and rest a while: for there were many coming and going, and they had no leisure so much as to eat" (Mk. 6:31).

I highly recommend my book, *"The Law of Recognition."* It contains a chapter listing "92 Facts You Should Know About Enemies."

You Must Identify Adversarial Relationships That Distract You From Your Goals.

～ 7 ～

YOUR GREATEST GOAL SHOULD BE KNOWING GOD.

The Goals Of God Are More Important Than Your's.

God has a Master Plan for your success. Nobody cares more about your goals and dreams than The Creator who has birthed them within you. But, you must never allow them to become a substitute for Him. Like Abraham, your loyalty and affection will be tested (Gen. 22:8-14).

God Is A Jealous God Who Will Not Tolerate The Worship Of Anything Else In Your Life. "For thou shalt worship no other god: for the Lord, Whose name is Jealous, is a jealous God: Lest thou make a covenant with the inhabitants of the land, and they go a whoring after their gods, and do sacrifice unto their gods, and one call thee, and thou eat of his sacrifice;" (Ex. 34:14,15).

God Is Greatly Concerned That Obedience Becomes Your Focus, Instead Of His Blessings. "Then thine heart be lifted up, and thou forget the Lord thy God, which brought thee forth out of the land of Egypt, from the house of bondage...And it shall be, if thou do at all forget the Lord thy God, and walk after other gods, and serve them, and worship them, I testify against you this day that ye shall surely perish" (Deut. 8:14,19).

Your Obedience Includes A Church Home Where

You Receive Spiritual Mentorship. "Not forsaking the assembling of ourselves together, as the manner of some is; but exhorting one another: and so much the more, as ye see the day approaching" (Heb. 10:25).

I am the son of a pastor. My father often warned his people to put God first in everything. He saw parents obsessed with their children's involvement with school sports and eventually stop coming to the Wednesday night services. He saw businesses flourish and their owners too busy to come to Sunday night services. Anything That Takes You Away From His Presence Is A Trap. Don't fall for it.

Many who prosper financially have failed miserably in their prayer life as their business became their "god."

Many who received the gift of children from God made their children their "god" and put sports and vacations ahead of their spiritual mentorship. The loss is deadly.

- ▶ Stay involved with your church.
- ▶ Respect the correction of your Shepherd and Pastor.
- ▶ Mentor your family in the Word of God.
- ▶ Keep your morning appointments with the Holy Spirit.
- ▶ Keep your word to others whatever the cost.
- ▶ Fight to maintain your integrity.

When you do, God will commit Himself to you and His success plans for you...will surely come to pass at the appointed time. "For I know the thoughts that I think toward you, saith the Lord, thoughts of peace, and not of evil, to give you an expected end. Then shall ye call upon Me, and ye shall go and pray unto

Me, and I will hearken unto you. And ye shall seek Me, and find Me, when ye shall search for Me with all your heart" (Jer. 29:11-13).

Your Greatest Goal Should Be Knowing God.

——— *My Closing Thought* ———

If this Wisdom book has blessed you, I'd love to hear from you! You may order additional copies for a friend, cell group, or associates at your workplace.

The Greatest Gift Of All...Is The Gift Of Wisdom.

Quantity Price List For
The Seeds Of Wisdom On Goal-Setting (B-127)

Quantity	Cost each	Discount	Quantity	Cost each	Discount
1-9 =	$5.00 ea.	Retail	2000-4999 =	$2.00 ea.	60%
10-499 =	$3.00 ea.	40%	5000-up	= Contact Office	
500-1999 =	$2.50 ea.	50%			

(Add 10% shipping all single titles.)

RECOMMENDED BOOKS AND TAPES:

"The Assignment (The Dream & The Destiny)" Vol. 1 *(151 Page Book)* B-74/$10

"The Assignment (The Anointing & The Adversity)" Vol. 2 *(143 Page Book)* B-75/$10

"The Assignment (The Trials & The Triumphs)" Vol. 3 *(160 Page Book)* B-97/$10

"The Assignment (The Pain & The Passion)" Vol. 4 *(143 Page Book)* B-98/$10

"The Leadership Secrets Of Jesus" *(221 Page Book)* B-91/$10

"The Law of Recognition" *(256 Page Book)* B-114/$10

"Wisdom for Winning" *(219 Page Book)* B-01/$10

"The Assignment" *(6-Tape Series)* TS-22/$30

Order Your *FREE* Wisdom Gift Catalog!

The Wisdom Center
P. O. Box 99
Denton, TX 76202
1-888-WISDOM-1
(1-888-947-3661)
Website:
www.thewisdomcenter.cc

Dear Friend,

You matter.

You are important to God. If you need special prayer, don't hesitate to write today.

My staff and I will pray for you. I will write you back.

God has brought us together for a reason.

Will you become my Monthly Faith Partner?

Your Seeds of Loving Support will bless so many....and birth uncommon increase in your own life.

When you sow, expect Four Scriptural Harvests:
► Uncommon Protection (Mal. 3:10,11)
► Uncommon Favor (Lk. 6:38)
► Uncommon Health (Isa. 58:8)
► Uncommon Financial Ideas (Deut. 8:18)

An Uncommon Seed Always Creates An Uncommon Harvest (Mk. 10:28-30).

Looking for your letter,

Mike Murdock

DECISION

Will You Accept Jesus As Your Personal Savior Today?

The Bible says, "That if thou shalt confess with thy mouth the Lord Jesus, and shalt believe in thine heart that God hath raised Him from the dead, thou shalt be saved" (Rom. 10:9).

Pray this prayer from your heart today!

"Dear Jesus, I believe that you died for me and rose again on the third day. I confess I am a sinner...I need Your love and forgiveness...Come into my heart. Forgive my sins. I receive Your eternal life. Confirm Your love by giving me peace, joy and supernatural love for others. Amen."

Clip and Mail

DR. MIKE MURDOCK

is in tremendous demand as one of the most dynamic speakers in America today.

More than 14,000 audiences in 38 countries have attended his meetings and seminars. Hundreds of invitations come to him from churches, colleges, and business corporations. He is a noted author of over 120 books, including the best sellers, *"The Leadership Secrets of Jesus"* and *"Secrets of the Richest Man Who Ever Lived."* Thousands view his weekly television program, *"Wisdom Keys with Mike Murdock."* Many have attended his Saturday School of Wisdom Breakfasts that he hosts in major cities of America.

☐ Yes, Mike! I made a decision to accept Christ as my personal Savior today. Please send me my free gift of your book, *"31 Keys to a New Beginning"* to help me with my new life in Christ. *(B-48)*

NAME _____ BIRTHDATE _____

ADDRESS _____

CITY _____ STATE ___ ZIP _____

PHONE _____ E-MAIL _____ *B-127*

Mail form to:

The Wisdom Center · P. O. Box 99 · Denton, TX 76202
1-888-WISDOM-1 (1-888-947-3661)
Website: www.thewisdomcenter.cc

My Gift Of Appreciation...
The Wisdom Commentary

The Wisdom Commentary includes
52 topics...for mentoring your
family every week of the year.

These topics include:

- Abilities
- Achievement
- Anointing
- Assignment
- Bitterness
- Blessing
- Career
- Change
- Children
- Dating
- Depression
- Discipline
- Divorce
- Dreams And Goals
- Enemy
- Enthusiasm
- Favor
- Finances
- Fools

- Giving
- Goal-Setting
- God
- Happiness
- Holy Spirit
- Ideas
- Intercession
- Jobs
- Loneliness
- Love
- Mentorship
- Ministers
- Miracles
- Mistakes
- Money
- Negotiation
- Prayer
- Problem-Solving
- Protégés

- Satan
- Secret Place
- Seed-Faith
- Self-Confidence
- Struggle
- Success
- Time-Management
- Understanding
- Victory
- Weaknesses
- Wisdom
- Word Of God
- Words
- Work

THE *Mike Murdock* COLLECTOR'S EDITION

The Wisdom Commentary of MIKE MURDOCK

THE **Wisdom**
Commentary

VOLUME 1

GIFT OF APPRECIATION
For Your
Sponsorship
Seed of $100
or More
B-136
GIFT OF APPRECIATION

My Gift Of Appreciation To My Sponsors!
...Those Who Sponsor One Square Foot In
The Completion Of The Wisdom Center!

Thank you so much for becoming a part of this wonderful project...The completion of The Wisdom Center
The total purchase and renovation cost of this facility (10,000 square feet) is just over $1,000,000. This
approximately $100 per square foot. **The Wisdom Commentary is my Gift of Appreciation for you**
Sponsorship Seed of $100...that sponsors one square foot of The Wisdom Center. Become a Sponsor! Yo
will love this Volume 1, of The Wisdom Commentary. It is my exclusive Gift of Appreciation for The Wisdo
Key Family who partners with me in the Work of God as a Sponsor.

 THE WISDOM CENTER P.O. Box 99, Denton, Texas 76202

─ Website: ─
WWW.THEWISDOMCENTER.CC

1-888-WISDOM
(1-888-947-3661

THE WISDOM CENTER

1-888-WISDOM-1 (1-888-947-3661)

Mon.-Fri.
8 AM-5 PM CST

visit us at:
www.thewisdomcenter.cc

PRODUCT NUMBER	PRODUCT DESCRIPTION	QTY	PRICE	TOTAL
				1
				2
				3
				4
				5
				6

	SubTotal	$ 7
	Canada ADD 20%	8
	S/H Add 10%	$ 9
	TOTAL	$ 10

My Seed Offering $ 11

Your Seed Faith Offering is used to support the MIKE MURDOCK Evangelistic Association, The Wisdom Center, and all its programs. Applicable law requires that we have the discretion to allocate donations in order to carry out our charitable purpose. In the event MMEA receives more funds for the project than needed, excess more funds will be used for another worthy outreach.

Name
Address
City _____ State _____ Zip
Phone _____ Email

Method of Payment
☐ Cash ☐ Check ☐ Visa ☐ MC ☐ Amex ☐ Discover

Card# _____

Birthday _____ MO _____ DAY

Expiration Date _____

Total Enclosed $ _____

Signature _____

(Sorry No C.O.D.'s)

B 127

Bookstore Discounts
(single titles only)

QTY.	DISCOUNT
1-9	Retail
10-499	40%
500-1999	50%
2000-4999	60%
5000 & Up	Contact Office

My Precious Partner,

Your Goals Are So Important To Me.

My Assignment is to help you achieve your dreams and goals...by sowing the Wisdom of God into your life.

That's why I wrote this explosive book on Goal-Setting...JUST FOR YOU. I have poured my heart into it... knowing that one Wisdom Key can solve a thousand problems in your life.

I am praying for you daily...in The Secret Place. Being your intercessor is very important to me.

Thank you for sowing your Seeds into this ministry. Your Seed is the Golden Secret to scheduling a Miracle Future. Sow Expectantly. Expect your Harvest to come back where you need it most.

Write me today...and tell me how this book helps you.

Your Faithful Intercessor,

Mike Murdock

P.S. When you sow your Seed into this ministry, target it toward the fulfillment of your dream. (Please use the postage paid envelope inside this book!) visit website www.thewisdomcenter.cc

WISDOM 12 PAK

THE MASTER SECRET OF LIFE IS WISDOM
Ignorance Is The Only True Enemy Capable Of Destroying You (Hosea 4:6, Proverbs 11:14)

▶ 1. MY PERSONAL DREAM BOOK	B143	$5.00
▶ 2. THE COVENANT OF FIFTY-EIGHT BLESSINGS	B47	$8.00
▶ 3. WISDOM, GOD'S GOLDEN KEY TO SUCCESS	B71	$7.00
▶ 4. SEEDS OF WISDOM ON THE HOLY SPIRIT	B116	$5.00
▶ 5. SEEDS OF WISDOM ON THE SECRET PLACE	B115	$5.00
▶ 6. SEEDS OF WISDOM ON THE WORD OF GOD	B117	$5.00
▶ 7. SEEDS OF WISDOM ON YOUR ASSIGNMENT	B122	$5.00
▶ 8. SEEDS OF WISDOM ON PROBLEM SOLVING	B118	$5.00
▶ 9. 101 WISDOM KEYS	B45	$7.00
▶ 10. 31 KEYS TO A NEW BEGINNING	B48	$7.00
▶ 11. THE PROVERBS 31 WOMAN	B49	$7.00
▶ 12. 31 FACTS ABOUT WISDOM	B46	$7.00

Wisdom Is The Principal Thing
Book Pak WBL-12 / $30
(A $73 Value!)
The Wisdom Center

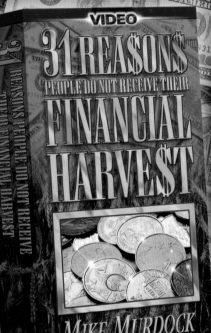

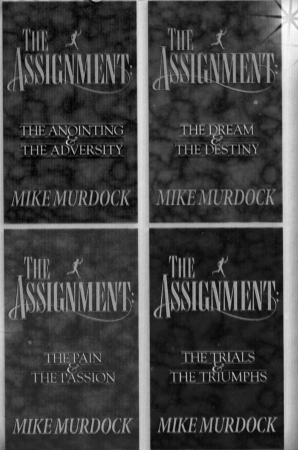

The Secret Place

Library Pak

Songs From The Secret Place

Over 40 Great Songs On 6 Music Tapes
Including "I'm In Love" / Love Songs From The Holy Spirit
Birthed In The Secret Place / Side A Is Dr. Mike Murdock
Singing / Side B Is Music Only For Your Personal Prayer Time

Seeds Of Wisdom On The Secret Place

4 Secrets The Holy Spirit Reveals In The Secret Place /
The Necessary Ingredients In Creating Your Secret Place /
10 Miracles That Will Happen In The Secret Place

Wisdom Is The Principal Thing
Book/Tape Pak
SP PAK-001 **/$30**
Six Audio Tapes & Two Books
(A $40 Value!)
The Wisdom Center

Seeds Of Wisdom On The Holy Spirit

The Protocol For Entering The Presence Of The Holy Spirit /
The Greatest Day Of My Life And What Made It So /
Power Keys For Developing Your Personal Relationship With The Holy Spirit

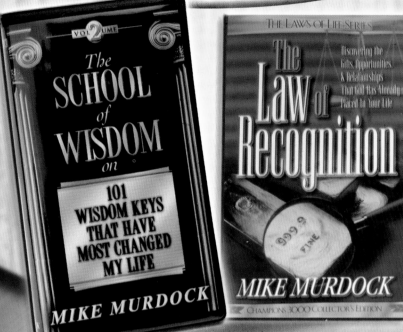

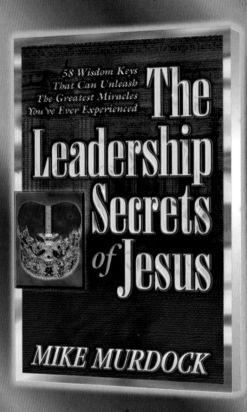

You Can Have It.

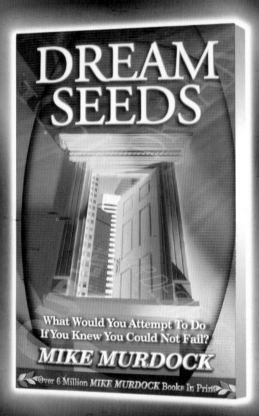

- ▸ Why Sickness Is Not The Will Of God

- ▸ How To Release The Powerful Forces That Guarantee Blessing

- ▸ The Incredible Role Of Your Memory And The Imagination

- ▸ The Hidden Power Of Imagination And How To Use It Properly

- ▸ The Difference Between The Love Of God And His Blessings

- ▸ 3 Steps In Increasing Your Faith

- ▸ 2 Rewards That Come When You Use Your Faith In God

- ▸ 7 Powerful Keys Concerning Your Faith

Dreams and desires begin as photographs within our hearts and minds - things that we want to happen in our future. God plants these pictures as invisible Seeds within us. God begins every miracle in your life with a Seed-picture... the invisible idea that gives birth to a visible blessing. In this teaching, you will discover your desires and how to concentrate on watering and nurturing the growth of your Dream-Seeds until you attain your God-given goals.

Wisdom Is The Principal Thing

Book B-11 / $9

Six Audio Tapes TS-2 / $30

The Wisdom Center

Where You Are Determines What Grows In You.

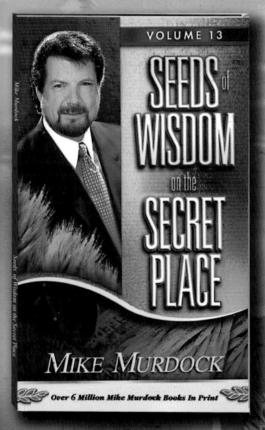

VOLUME 13

SEEDS of WISDOM on the SECRET PLACE

MIKE MURDOCK

Over 6 Million Mike Murdock Books In Print

▸ 4 Secrets The Holy Spirit Reveals In The Secret Place

▸ Master Keys In Cultivating An Effective Prayer Life

▸ The Necessary Ingredients In Creating Your Secret Place

▸ 10 Miracles That Will Happen In The Secret Place

ORDER TODAY!
www.thewisdomcenter.cc

1-888-WISDOM-1
(1-888-947-3661)

THE WISDOM CENTER • P.O. Box 99 • Denton, Texas 76202

K

Run To Win.

- 10 Ingredients For Success
- 10 Lies Many People Believe About Money
- 20 Keys For Winning At Work
- 20 Keys To A Better Marriage
- 3 Facts Every Parent Should Remember
- 5 Steps Out Of Depression
- The Greatest Wisdom Principle I Ever Learned
- 7 Keys To Answered Prayer
- God's Master Golden Key To Total Success
- The Key To Understanding Life

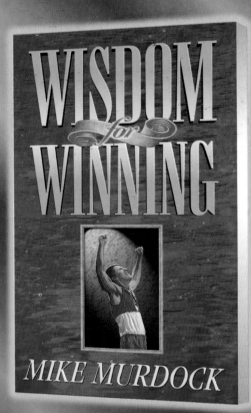

WISDOM *for* **WINNING**

MIKE MURDOCK

Everyone needs to feel they have achieved something with their life. When we stop producing, loneliness and laziness will choke all enthusiasm from our living. What would you like to be doing? What are you doing about it? Get started on a project in your life. Start building on your dreams. Resist those who would control and change your personal goals. Get going with this powerful teaching and reach your life goals!

Wisdom Is The Principal Thing

Book B-01 / **$10**

Six Audio Tapes TS-01 / **$30**

The Wisdom Center

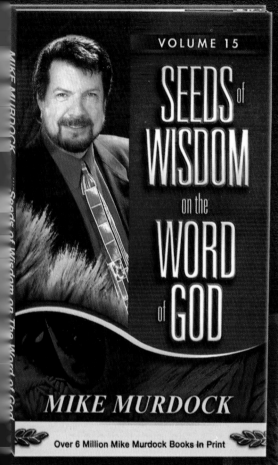

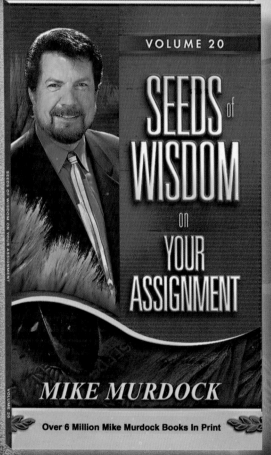

WISDOM COLLECTION

8

SECRETS OF THE UNCOMMON MILLIONAIRE

1. The Uncommon Millionaire Conference Vol. 1 (Six Cassettes)
2. The Uncommon Millionaire Conference Vol. 2 (Six Cassettes)
3. The Uncommon Millionaire Conference Vol. 3 (Six Cassettes)
4. The Uncommon Millionaire Conference Vol. 4 (Six Cassettes)
5. 31 Reasons People Do Not Receive Their Financial Harvest (256 Page Book)
6. Secrets of the Richest Man Who Ever Lived (178 Page Book)
7. 12 Seeds Of Wisdom Books On 12 Topics
8. The Gift Of Wisdom For Leaders Desk Calendar
9. 101 Wisdom Keys On Tape (Audio Tape)
10. In Honor Of The Holy Spirit (Music Cassette)
11. 365 Memorization Scriptures On The Word Of God (Audio Cassette)